LOVE SONNETS

ELIZABETH BARRETT
BROWNING

LOVE SONNETS

ELIZABETH BARRETT BROWNING

BARNES & NOBLE
BOOKS
NEW YORK

This edition published by Marboro Books Corp.,
a division of Barnes & Noble, Inc.

1993 Barnes & Noble Books

Book design by Charles Ziga, Ziga Design

ISBN 1-56619-037-1

Printed and bound in the United States of America

M 9 8 7 6 5 4

CONTENTS

Introduction

This book of love sonnets unites Elizabeth Barrett Browning's celebrated *Sonnets from the Portuguese* with earlier poems written prior to her first correspondence with Robert Browning. These early sonnets, published in 1844 as part of a book entitled *Poems,* are works expressing a wide vision attained through meditation and seclusion. A line from "The Prisoner" says much of her life at this time: *Nature's lute/Sounds on behind this door so closely shut.* The general theme of these poems is the expression of a spiritual, almost religious love toward God, which Elizabeth saw as part of the *solemn responsibilities of the poet.* Yet, if Elizabeth did lead a cloistered life, it was not one of total seclusion. In her own time she was recognized as one of England's finest poets. She corresponded with such luminaries as Wordsworth, Carlyle, and Tennyson, and was even thought of so highly that she was considered as a possible poet laureate of England after the death of William Wordsworth. Although Robert Browning's name is more widely known today, in their own time Elizabeth had the greater recognition, for Robert's work largely existed for his fellow contemporary poets. They wrote each other often, but they were not to actually meet for some time after their first correspondence. The following lines from one of the *Sonnets from the Portuguese,* the first poem she wrote after recognizing Robert's sincere love for her, tells much of the transformation that his love would make upon her life.

> . . . a mystic Shape did move
> Behind me, did drew backwards by the hair
> And a voice said in mastery as I strove,
> "Guess now who holds thee?"—"Death," I said.
>   But there,
> The silver answer rang,—"Not Death, but Love."

This spiritual, celestial devotion that changed in a matter of weeks to a personal, passionate love is captured throughout the *Sonnets from the Portuguese.*

Elizabeth and Robert Browning had what observers called a "successful" marriage. They worked well together as a couple; he admired her work, and she would be even more disappointed than he when his poems did not generate the recognition that she felt they deserved. They did disagree on such subjects as diverse as the politics of Napoleon the Third to the fashions that their child, Pen, should wear. But these arguments were never to impede their relationship seriously, for some things simply did not enter the love they held between each other. Neither over-sentimentalized nor over-romanticized, the Browning's marriage was that of two poets very conscious of their art and how it related to their experiences and reflections. Their marriage could not be viewed in the sarcastic light of Byron's words that *moral centaur, man and wife,* but was instead, as Elizabeth would write, *like riding an enchanted horse*—not the monstrous horse of the centaur, but Pegasus, the horse of poets. In the *Sonnets from the Portuguese,* Elizabeth communicates the various aspects of her love for Robert through metaphors and symbols for the aspects of life, death, the heart and soul, and the sun and moon. Their extremely personal love could in this way be made public without causing offense or envy. Yet, even still, she cleverly thought to bring these sonnets more into the public realm by calling them translations of Portuguese poems. This was a play on Robert's intimate name for her, "my little

Portuguese," because of her olive complexion, as well as a tribute to his early admiration of her poem "Catarina to Camoëns," which describes the great love of the Portuguese poet Camoëns.

As the unique love expressed in the *Sonnets from the Portuguese* ennoblizes the reader, it also brings to the forefront Elizabeth's pained and reluctant struggle to submit herself to the demands and universal aspects of this *love for love's sake only.* Often she rejects this love and the love of her husband only to remake what she just declined. This painful, self-prescribed process of breaking and remaking vows brought her to experience fully both the attraction and the repulsion in her love for Robert. Thus, the *Sonnets from the Portuguese* records an intense spiritual exercise and exploration of Elizabeth's emotions during her courtship and betrothal. It is no wonder Robert was both astonished and proud of his wife's love for him. For he knew himself to be loved so perfectly through the wonder of her art that their love would defy even death.

—ROBERT YAGLEY

1993

SONNETS
FROM THE
PORTUGUESE

∽ I ∾

I thought once how Theocritus had sung
Of the sweet years, the dear and wished-for years,
Who each one in a gracious hand appears
To bear a gift for mortals, old or young:
And, as I mused it in his antique tongue,
I saw, in gradual vision through my tears,
The sweet, sad years, the melancholy years,
Those of my own life, who by turns had flung
A shadow across me. Straightway I was 'ware,
So weeping, how a mystic shape did move
Behind me, and drew me backward by the hair;
And a voice said in mastery, while I strove,—
"Guess now who holds thee!"—"Death" I said. But there
The silver answer rang,—"Not Death, but Love."

*B*ut only three in all God's universe
Have heard this word thou hast said,—Himself, beside
Thee speaking, and me listening! and replied
One of us . . . *that* was God . . . and laid the curse
So darkly on my eyelids, as to amerce
My sight from seeing thee,—that if I had died,
The death-weights, placed there, would have signified
Less absolute exclusion. "Nay" is worse
From God than from all others, O my friend!
Men could not part us with their worldly jars,
Nor the seas change us, nor the tempests bend;
Our hands would touch for all the mountain-bars:
And, heaven being rolled between us at the end,
We should but vow the faster for the stars.

⌇ III ⌇

*U*nlike are we, unlike, O princely Heart!
Unlike our uses and our destinies.
Our ministering two angels look surprise
On one another, as they strike athwart
Their wings in passing. Thou, bethink thee, art
A guest for queens to social pageantries,
With gages from a hundred brighter eyes
Than tears even can make mine, to play thy part
Of chief musician. What hast *thou* to do
With looking from the lattice-lights at me,
A poor, tired, wandering singer, singing through
The dark, and leaning up a cypress tree?
The chrism is on thine head, on mine, the dew,—
And Death must dig the level where these agree.

∽ IV ∽

*T*hou hast thy calling to some palace-floor,
Most gracious singer of high poems! where
The dancers will break footing, from the care
Of watching up thy pregnant lips for more.
And dost thou lift this house's latch too poor
For hand of thine? and canst thou think and bear
To let thy music drop here unaware
In folds of golden fullness at my door?
Look up and see the casement broken in,
The bats and owlets builders in the roof!
My cricket chirps against thy mandolin.
Hush, call no echo up in further proof
Of desolation! there's a voice within
That weeps . . . as thou must sing . . . alone, aloof.

I lift my heavy heart up solemnly,
As once Electra her sepulchral urn,
And, looking in thine eyes, I overturn
The ashes at thy feet. Behold and see
What a great heap of grief lay hid in me,
And how the red wild sparkles dimly burn
Through the ashen greyness. If thy foot in scorn
Could tread them out to darkness utterly,
It might be well perhaps. But if instead
Thou wait beside me for the wind to blow
The grey dust up . . . those laurels on thine head,
O my Belovèd, will not shield thee so,
That none of all the fires shall scorch and shred
The hair beneath. Stand farther off then! go!

*G*o from me. Yet I feel that I shall stand
Henceforward in thy shadow. Nevermore
Alone upon the threshold of my door
Of individual life, I shall command
The uses of my soul, nor lift my hand
Serenely in the sunshine as before,
Without the sense of that which I forbore—
Thy touch upon the palm. The widest land
Doom takes to part us, leaves thy heart in mine
With pulses that beat double. What I do
And what I dream include thee, as the wine
Must taste of its own grapes. And when I sue
God for myself, He hears that name of thine,
And sees within my eyes the tears of two.

*T*he face of all the world is changed, I think,
Since first I heard the footsteps of thy soul
Move still, oh, still, beside me, as they stole
Betwixt me and the dreadful outer brink
Of obvious death, where I, who thought to sink,
Was caught up into love, and taught the whole
Of life in a new rhythm. The cup of dole
God gave for baptism, I am fain to drink,
And praise its sweetness, Sweet, with thee anear.
The names of country, heaven, are changed away
For where thou art or shalt be, there or here;
And this . . . this lute and song . . . loved yesterday,
(The singing angels know) are only dear
Because thy name moves right in what they say.

*W*hat can I give thee back, O liberal
And princely giver, who hast brought the gold
And purple of thine heart, unstained, untold,
And laid them on the outside of the wall
For such as I to take or leave withal,
In unexpected largesse? am I cold,
Ungrateful, that for these most manifold
High gifts, I render nothing back at all?
Not so; not cold,—but very poor instead.
Ask God who knows. For frequent tears have run
The colors from my life, and left so dead
And pale a stuff, if it were not fitly done
To give the same as pillow to thy head.
Go farther! let it serve to trample on.

~ IX ~

*C*an it be right to give what I can give?
To let thee sit beneath the fall of tears
As salt as mine, and hear the sighing years
Re-sighing on my lips renunciative
Through those infrequent smiles which fail to live
For all thy adjurations? O my fears,
That this can scarce be right! We are not peers
So to be lovers; and I own, and grieve,
That givers of such gifts as mine are, must
Be counted with the ungenerous. Out, alas!
I will not soil thy purple with my dust,
Nor breathe my poison on thy Venice-glass,
Nor give thee any love, which were unjust.
Belovèd, I only love thee! let it pass.

❦ X ❦

Yet, love, mere love, is beautiful indeed
And worthy of acceptation. Fire is bright,
Let temple burn, or flax; an equal light
Leaps in the flame from cedar-plank or weed:
And love is fire. And when I say at need
I love thee . . . mark! . . . *I love thee*—in thy sight
I stand transfigured, glorified aright,
With conscience of the new rays that proceed
Out of my face toward thine. There's nothing low
In love, when love the lowest: meanest creatures
Who love God, God accepts while loving so.
And what I *feel,* across the inferior features
Of what I *am,* doth flash itself, and show
How that great work of Love enhances Nature's.

*A*nd therefore if to love can be desert,
I am not all unworthy. Cheeks as pale
As these you see, and trembling knees that fail
To bear the burden of a heavy heart,—
This weary minstrel-life that once was girt
To climb Aornus, and can scarce avail
To pipe now 'gainst the valley nightingale
A melancholy music,—why advert
To these things? O Belovèd, it is plain
I am not of thy worth nor for thy place!
And yet, because I love thee, I obtain
From that same love this vindicating grace
To live on still in love, and yet in vain,—
To bless thee, yet renounce thee to thy face.

*I*ndeed this very love which is my boast,
And which, when rising up from breast to brow,
Doth crown me with a ruby large enow
To draw men's eyes and prove the inner cost,—
This love even, all my worth, to the uttermost,
I should not love withal, unless that thou
Hadst set me an example, shown me how,
When first thine earnest eyes with mine were crossed
And love called love. And thus, I cannot speak
Of love even, as a good thing of my own:
Thy soul hath snatched up mine all faint and weak,
And placed it by thee on a golden throne,—
And that I love (O soul, we must be meek!)
Is by thee only, whom I love alone.

⟿ XIII ⟿

*A*nd wilt thou have me fashion into speech
The love I bear thee, finding words enough,
And hold the torch out, while the winds are rough
Between our faces, to cast light on each?—
I drop it at thy feet. I cannot teach
My hand to hold my spirit so far off
From myself—me—that I should bring the proof
In words, of love hid in me out of reach.
Nay, let the silence of my womanhood
Commend my woman-love to thy belief,—
Seeing that I stand unwon, however wooed,
And rend the garment of my life, in brief,
By a most dauntless, voiceless fortitude,
Lest one touch of this heart convey its grief.

*I*f thou must love me, let it be for nought
Except for love's sake only. Do not say
"I love her for her smile—her look—her way
Of speaking gently,—for a trick of thought
That falls in well with mine, and certes brought
A sense of pleasant ease on such a day"—
For these things in themselves, Belovèd, may
Be changed, or change for thee,—and love,
    so wrought.
May be unwrought so. Neither love me for
Thine own dear pity's wiping my cheeks dry,—
A creature might forget to weep, who bore
Thy comfort long, and lose thy love thereby!
But love me for love's sake, that evermore
Thou may'st love on, through love's eternity.

∽ XV ∽

*A*ccuse me not, beseech thee, that I wear
Too calm and sad a face in front of thine;
For we two look two ways, and cannot shine
With the same sunlight on our brow and hair.
On me thou lookest with no doubting care,
As on a bee shut in a crystalline;
Since sorrow hath shut me safe in love's divine,
And to spread wing and fly in the outer air
Were most impossible failure, if I strove
To fail so. But I look on thee—on thee—
Beholding, besides love, the end of love,
Hearing oblivion beyond memory;
As one who sits and gazes from above,
Over the rivers to the bitter sea.

∾ XVI ∾

*A*nd yet, because thou overcomest so,
Because thou art more noble and like a king,
Thou canst prevail against my fears and fling
Thy purple round me, till my heart shall grow
Too close against thine heart henceforth to know
How it shook when alone. Why, conquering
May prove as lordly and complete a thing
In lifting upward, as in crushing low!
And as a vanquished soldier yields his sword
To one who lifts him from the bloody earth,
Even so, Belovèd, I at last record,
Here ends my strife. If *thou* invite me forth,
I rise above abasement at the word.
Make thy love larger to enlarge my worth!

*M*y poet, thou canst touch on all the notes
God set between His After and Before,
And strike up and strike off the general roar
Of the rushing worlds a melody that floats
In a serene air purely. Antidotes
Of medicated music, answering for
Mankind's forlornest uses, thou canst pour
From thence into their ears. God's will devotes
Thine to such ends, and mine to wait on thine.
How, Dearest, wilt thou have me for most use?
A hope, to sing by gladly? or a fine
Sad memory, with thy songs to interfuse?
A shade, in which to sing—or palm or pine?
A grave, on which to rest from singing? Choose.

∽ XVIII ∼

*I*never gave a lock of hair away
To a man, Dearest, except this to thee,
Which now upon my fingers thoughtfully
I ring out to the full brown length and say
"Take it." My day of youth went yesterday;
My hair no longer bounds to my foot's glee,
Nor plant I it from rose or myrtle-tree,
As girls do, any more: it only may
Now shade on two pale cheeks the mark of tears,
Taught drooping from the head that hangs aside
Through sorrow's trick. I thought the funeral-shears
Would take this first, but Love is justified—
Take it thou,—finding pure, from all those years,
The kiss my mother left here when she died.

∽ XIX ∽

*T*he soul's Rialto hath its merchandise;
I barter curl for curl upon that mart,
And from my poet's forehead to my heart
Receive this lock which outweighs argosies,—
As purely black, as erst to Pindar's eyes
The dim purpureal tresses gloomed athwart
The nine white Muse-brows. For this counterpart . . .
The bay crown's shade, Belovèd, I surmise,
Still lingers on thy curl, it is so black!
Thus, with a fillet of smooth-kissing breath,
I tie the shadows safe from gliding back
And lay the gift where nothing hindereth;
Here on my heart, as on thy brow, to lack
No natural heat till mine grows cold in death.

∽ XX ∽

*S*ay over again, and yet once over again,
That thou dost love me. Though the word repeated
Should seem a "cuckoo-song," as thou dost treat it,
Remember, never to the hill or plain,
Valley and wood, without her cuckoo-strain,
Comes the fresh Spring in all her green completed.
Belovèd, I, amid the darkness greeted
By a doubtful spirit-voice, in that doubt's pain
Cry, "Speak once more—thou lovest!" Who can fear
Too many stars, though each in heaven shall roll,
Too many flowers, though each shall crown the year?
Say thou dost love me, love me, love me—toll
The silver iterance!—only minding, Dear,
To love me also in silence with thy soul.

XXI

*B*elovèd, my Belovèd, when I think
That thou wast in the world a year ago,
What time I sat alone here in the snow
And saw no footprint, heard the silence sink
No moment at thy voice, but, link by link,
Went counting all my chains as if that so
They never could fall off at any blow
Struck by thy possible hand,—why, thus I drink
Of life's great cup of wonder! Wonderful
Never to feel thee thrill the day or night
With personal act or speech,—nor ever cull
Some prescience of thee with the blossoms white
Thou sawest growing! Atheists are as dull,
Who cannot guess God's presence out of sight.

*W*hen our two souls stand up erect and strong,
Face to face, silent, drawing nigh and nigher,
Until the lengthening wings break into fire
At either curvèd point,—what bitter wrong
Can the earth do to us, that we should not long
Be here contented? Think! In mounting higher,
The angels would press on us and aspire
To drop some golden orb of perfect song
Into our deep, dear silence. Let us stay
Rather on earth, Belovèd,—where the unfit
Contrarious moods of men recoil away
And isolate pure spirits, and permit
A place to stand and love in for a day,
With darkness and the death-hour rounding it.

*I*s it indeed so? If I lay here dead,
Wouldst thou miss any life in losing mine?
And would the sun for thee more coldly shine
Because of grave-damps falling round my head?
I marveled, my Belovèd, when I read
Thy thought so in the letter. I am thine—
But . . . *so* much to thee? Can I pour thy wine
While my hands tremble? Then my soul, instead
Of dreams of death, resumes life's lower range.
Then, love me, Love! Look on me—breathe on me!
As brighter ladies do not count it strange,
For love, to give up acres and degree,
I yield the grave for thy sake, and exchange
My near sweet view of heaven, for earth with thee!

∽ XXIV ∽

*L*et the world's sharpness, like a clasping knife,
Shut in upon itself and do no harm
In this close hand of Love, now soft and warm,
And let us hear no sound of human strife
After the click of the shutting. Life to life —
I lean upon thee, Dear, without alarm,
And feel as safe as guarded by a charm
Against the stab of worldlings, who if rife
Are weak to injure. Very whitely still
The lilies of our lives may reassure
Their blossoms from their roots, accessible
Alone to heavenly dews that drop not fewer;
Growing straight, out of man's reach, on the hill.
God only, who made us rich, can make us poor.

∽ XXV ∽

A heavy heart, Belovèd, have I borne
From year to year until I saw thy face,
And sorrow after sorrow took the place
Of all those natural joys as lightly worn
As the stringèd pearls, each lifted in its turn
By a beating heart at dance-time. Hopes apace
Were changed to long despairs, till God's own grace
Could scarcely lift above the world forlorn
My heavy heart. Then *thou* didst bid me bring
And let it drop adown thy calmly great
Deep being! Fast it sinketh, as a thing
Which its own nature does precipitate,
While thine doth close above it, mediating
Betwixt the stars and the unaccomplished fate.

I lived with visions for my company
Instead of men and women, years ago,
And found them gentle mates, nor thought to know
A sweeter music than they played to me.
But soon their trailing purple was not free
Of this world's dust, their lutes did silent grow,
And I myself grew faint and blind below
Their vanishing eyes. Then thou didst come, to be,
Belovèd, what they seemed. Their shining fronts,
Their songs, their splendors, (better, yet the same,
As river-water hallowed into fonts)
Met in thee, and from out thee overcame
My soul with satisfaction of all wants:
Because God's gifts put man's best dreams to shame.

*M*y own Belovèd, who has lifted me
From this drear flat of earth where I was thrown,
And, in betwixt the languid ringlets, blown
A life-breath, till the forehead hopefully
Shines out again, as all the angels see,
Before thy saving kiss! My own, my own,
Who camest to me when the world was gone,
And I who looked for only God, found *thee!*
I find thee; I am safe, and strong, and glad.
As one who stands in dewless asphodel,
Looks backward on the tedious time he had
In the upper life,— so I, with bosom-swell,
Make witness, here, between the good and bad,
That Love, as strong as Death, retrieves as well.

∽ XXVIII ∽

*M*y letters! all dead paper, mute and white!
And yet they seem alive and quivering
Against my tremulous hands which loose the string
And let them drop down on my knee tonight.
This said,—he wished to have me in his sight
Once, as a friend: this fixed a day in Spring
To come and touch my hand . . . a simple thing,
Yet I wept for it!—this . . . the paper's light . . .
Said, *Dear, I love thee;* and I sank and quailed
As if God's future thundered on my past.
This said, *I am thine*—and so its ink has paled
With lying at my heart that beat too fast.
And this . . . O Love, thy words have ill availed
If, what this said, I dared repeat at last!

∽ XXIX ∽

I think of thee!—my thoughts do twine and bud
About thee, as wild vines, about a tree,
Put out broad leaves, and soon there's nought to see
Except the straggling green which hides the wood.
Yet, O my palm-tree, be it understood
I will not have my thoughts instead of thee
Who art dearer, better! Rather, instantly
Renew thy presence; as a strong tree should,
Rustle thy boughs and set thy trunk all bare,
And let these bands of greenery which insphere thee,
Drop heavily down,—burst, shattered everywhere!
Because, in this deep joy to see and hear thee
And breathe within thy shadow a new air,
I do not think of thee—I am too near thee.

∽ XXX ∾

I see thine image through my tears tonight,
And yet today I saw thee smiling. How
Refer the cause?—Belovèd, is it thou
Or I, who makes me sad? The acolyte
Amid the chanted joy and thankful rite
May so fall flat, with pale insensate brow,
On the altar-stair. I hear thy voice and vow,
Perplexed, uncertain, since thou art out of sight,
As he, in his swooning ears, the choir's amen.
Belovèd, dost thou love? or did I see all
The glory as I dreamed, and fainted when
Too vehement light dilated my ideal,
For my soul's eyes? Will that light come again,
As now these tears come—falling hot and real?

∽ XXXI ∽

*T*hou comest! all is said without a word,
I sit beneath thy looks, as children do
In the noon-sun, with souls that tremble through
Their happy eyelids from an unaverred
Yet prodigal inward joy. Behold, I erred
In that last doubt! and yet I cannot rue
The sin most, but the occasion—that we two
Should for a moment stand unministered
By a mutual presence. Ah, keep near and close,
Thou dove-like help! and, when my fears would rise,
With thy broad heart serenely interpose:
Brood down with thy divine sufficiencies
These thoughts which tremble when bereft of those,
Like callow birds left desert to the skies.

∽ XXXII ∽

*T*he first time that the sun rose on thine oath
To love, I looked forward to the moon
To slacken all those bonds which seemed too soon
And quickly tied to make a lasting troth.
Quick-loving hearts, I thought, may quickly loathe;
And, looking on myself, I seemed not one
For such man's love!—more like an out-of-tune
Worn viol, a good singer would be wroth
To spoil his song with, and which, snatched in haste,
Is laid down at the first ill-sounding note.
I did not wrong myself so, but I placed
A wrong on *thee*. For perfect strains may float
'Neath master-hands, from instruments defaced,—
And great souls, at one stroke, may do and doat.

∽ XXXIII ∽

*Y*es, call me by my pet-name! let me hear
The name I used to run at, when a child,
From innocent play, and leave the cowslips piled,
To glance up in some face that proved me dear
With the look of its eyes. I miss the clear
Fond voices which, being drawn and reconciled
Into the music of Heaven's undefiled,
Call me no longer. Silence on the bier,
While I call God — call God! — so let thy mouth
Be heir to those who are now exanimate.
Gather the north flowers to complete the south,
And catch the early love up in the late.
Yes, call me by that name, — and I, in truth,
With the same heart, will answer and not wait.

❧ XXXIV ❧

With the same heart, I said, I'll answer thee
As those, when thou shalt call me by my name—
Lo, the vain promise! is the same, the same,
Perplexed and ruffled by life's strategy?
When called before, I told how hastily
I dropped my flowers or brake off from a game,
To run and answer with the smile that came
At play last moment, and went on with me
Through my obedience. When I answer now,
I drop a grave thought, break from solitude;
Yet still my heart goes to thee—ponder how—
Not as to a single good, but all my good!
Lay thy hand on it, best one, and allow
That no child's foot could run fast as this blood.

～ XXXV ～

*I*f I leave all for thee, wilt thou exchange
And be all to me? Shall I never miss
Home-talk and blessing and the common kiss
That comes to each in turn, nor count it strange,
When I look up, to drop on a new range
Of walls and floors, another home than this?
Nay, wilt thou fill that place by me which is
Filled by dead eyes too tender to know change?
That's hardest. If to conquer love, has tried,
To conquer grief, tries more, as all things prove,
For grief indeed is love and grief beside.
Alas, I have grieved so I am hard to love.
Yet love me—wilt thou? Open thine heart wide,
And fold within, the wet wings of thy dove.

～ XXXVI ～

*W*hen we first met and loved, I did not build
Upon the event with marble. Could it mean
To last, a love set pendulous between
Sorrow and sorrow? Nay, I rather thrilled,
Distrusting every light that seemed to gild
The onward path, and feared to over-lean
A finger even. And, though I have grown serene
And strong since then, I think that God has willed
A still renewable fear . . . O love, O troth . . .
Lest these enclaspèd hands should never hold,
This mutual kiss drop down between us both
As an unowned thing, once the lips being cold,
And Love be false! if *he,* to keep one oath,
Must lose one joy, by his life's star foretold.

∽ XXXVII ∽

*P*ardon, oh, pardon, that my soul should make
Of all that strong divineness which I know
For thine and thee, an image only so
Formed of the sand, and fit to shift and break.
It is that distant years which did not take
Thy sovranty, recoiling with a blow,
Have forced my swimming brains to undergo
Their doubt and dread, and blindly to forsake
Thy purity of likeness and distort
Thy worthiest love to a worthless counterfeit.
As if a shipwrecked Pagan, safe in port,
His guardian sea-god to commemorate,
Should set a sculptured porpoise, gills a-snort
And vibrant tail, within the temple-gate.

*F*irst time he kissed me, he but only kissed
The fingers of this hand wherewith I write;
And ever since, it grew more clean and white,
Slow to world-greetings, quick with its "Oh, list,"
When the angels speak. A ring of amethyst
I could not wear here, plainer to my sight,
Than that first kiss. The second passed in height
The first, and sought the forehead, and half missed,
Half falling on the hair. O beyond meed!
That was the chrism of love, which love's own crown,
With sanctifying sweetness, did precede.
The third upon my lips was folded down
In perfect, purple state; since when, indeed,
I have been proud and said, "My love, my own."

⤳ XXXIX ⤳

*B*ecause thou hast the power and own'st the grace
To look through and behind this mask of me,
(Against which, years have beat thus blanchingly
With their rains,) and behold my soul's true face,
The dim and weary witness of life's race,—
Because thou hast the faith and love to see,
Through that same soul's distracting lethargy,
The patient angel waiting for a place
In the new Heavens,—because nor sin nor woe,
Nor God's infliction, nor death's neighborhood,
Nor all which others viewing, turn to go,
Nor all which makes me tired of all, self-viewed,—
Nothing repels thee . . . Dearest, teach me so
To pour out gratitude, as thou dost, good!

❧ XL ❧

*O*h, yes! they love through all this world of ours!
I will not gainsay love, called love forsooth.
I have heard love talked in my early youth,
And since, not so long back but that the flowers
Then gathered, smell still. Mussulmans and Giaours
Throw kerchiefs at a smile, and have no ruth
For any weeping. Polypheme's white tooth
Slips on the nut if, after frequent showers,
The shell is over-smooth,—and not so much
Will turn the thing called love, aside to hate
Or else to oblivion. But thou art not such
A lover, my Belovèd! thou canst wait
Through sorrow and sickness, to bring souls to touch,
And think it soon when others cry "too late."

∽ XLI ∼

I thank all who have loved me in their hearts,
With thanks and love from mine. Deep thanks to all
Who paused a little near the prison-wall
To hear my music in its louder parts
Ere they went onward, each one to the mart's
Or temple's occupation, beyond call.
But thou, who, in my voice's sink and fall
When the sob took it, thy divinest Art's
Own instrument didst drop down at thy foot
To hearken what I said between my tears . . .
Instruct me how to thank thee! Oh, to shoot
My soul's full meaning into future years,
That *they* should lend it utterance, and salute
Love that endures, from Life that disappears!

*M*y future will not copy fair my past—
I wrote that once; and thinking at my side
My ministering life-angel justified
The word by his appealing look upcast
To the white throne of God, I turned at last,
And there, instead, saw thee, not unallied
To angels in thy soul! Then I, long tried
By natural ills, received the comfort fast,
While budding, at thy sight, my pilgrim's staff
Gave out green leaves with morning dews impearled.
I seek no copy now of life's first half:
Leave here the pages with long musing curled,
And write me new my future's epigraph,
New angel mine, unhoped for in the world!

∽ XLIII ∽

*H*ow do I love thee? Let me count the ways.
I love thee to the depth and breadth and height
My soul can reach, when feeling out of sight
For the ends of Being and ideal Grace.
I love thee to the level of everyday's
Most quiet need, by sun and candle-light.
I love thee freely, as men strive for Right;
I love thee purely, as they turn from Praise.
I love thee with the passion put to use
In my old griefs, and with my childhood's faith.
I love thee with a love I seemed to lose
With my lost saints,—I love thee with the breath,
Smiles, tears, of all my life!—and, if God choose,
I shall but love thee better after death.

ᗞ XLIV ᗞ

*B*elovèd, thou hast brought me many flowers
Plucked in the garden, all the Summer through
And Winter, and it seemed as if they grew
In their close room, nor missed the sun and showers.
So, in the like name of that love of ours,
Take back these thoughts which here unfolded too,
And which on warm and cold days I withdrew
From my heart's ground. Indeed, those beds
    and bowers
Be overgrown with bitter weeds and rue,
And wait thy weeding; yet here's eglantine,
Here's ivy!—take them, as I used to do
Thy flowers, and keep them where they shall not pine.
Instruct thine eyes to keep their colors true,
And tell thy soul, their roots are left in mine.

EARLY
POEMS

PERPLEXED MUSIC

*E*xperience, like a pale musician, holds
A dulcimer of patience in his hand
Whence harmonies we cannot understand,
Of God's will in His worlds, the strain unfolds
In sad perplexed minors. Deathly colds
Fall on us while we hear and countermand
Our sanguine heart back from the fancyland
With nightingales in visionary wolds.
We murmur,—'Where is any certain tune
Of measured music, in such notes as these?'—
But angels, leaning from the golden seat,
Art not so minded: their fine ear hath won
The issue of complete cadences;
And, smiling down the stars, they whisper—SWEET.

GRIEF

I tell you, hopeless grief is passionless—
That only men incredulous of despair,
Half-taught in anguish, through the midnight air
Beat upward to God's throne in loud access
Of shrieking and reproach. Full desertness
In souls as countries, lieth silent-bare
Under the blanching, vertical eye-glare
Of the absolute Heavens. Deep-hearted man, express
Grief for thy Dead in silence like to death;
Most like a monumental statue set
In everlasting watch and moveless wo,
Till itself crumble to the dust beneath.
Touch it: the marble eyelids are not wet—
If it could weep, it could arise and go.

COMFORT

*S*peak low to me, my Saviour, low and sweet
From out the hallelujahs, sweet and low,
Lest I should fear and fall, and miss thee so
Who art not missed by any that entreat.
Speak to me as to Mary at thy feet—
And if no precious gums my hands bestow,
Let my tears drop like amber, while I go
In reach of thy divinest voice complete
In humanest affection—thus in sooth,
To lose the sense of losing! As a child,
Whose song-bird seeds the wood for evermore,
Is sung to in its stead by mother's mouth;
Till, sinking on her breast, love-reconciled,
He sleeps the faster that he wept before.

PAIN IN PLEASURE

A thought lay like a flower upon mine heart,
And drew around it other thoughts like bees
For multitude and thirst of sweetnesses;
Whereat rejoicing, I desired the art
Of the Greek whistler, who to wharf and mart
Could lure those insect swarms from orange-trees,
That I might hive with me such thoughts, and please
My soul so, always. Foolish counterpart
Of a weak man's vain wishes! while I spoke,
The thought I called a flower, grew nettle-rough—
The thoughts, called bees, stung me to festering.
Oh, entertain (cried Reason, as she woke,)
Your best and gladdest thoughts but long enough
And they will all prove sad enough to sting.

WORK

What are we set on earth for? Say, to toil—
Nor seek to leave thy tending of the vines,
For all the heat o' day, till it declines,
And Death's mild curfew shall from work assoil.
God did anoint thee with his odorous oil,
To wrestle, not to reign; and He assigns
All thy tears over, like pure crystallines,
For younger fellow-workers of the soil
To wear for amulets. So others shall
Take patience, labor, to their heart, and hand,
From thy hand, and thy heart, and thy brave cheer,
And God's grace fructify through thee to all.
The least flower, with a brimming cup, may stand
And share its dew-drop with another near.

CHEERFULNESS TAUGHT
BY REASON

I think we are too ready with complaint
In this fair world of God's. Had we no hope
Indeed beyond the zenith and the slope
Of yon grey bank of sky, we might be faint
To muse upon eternity's constraint
Round our aspirant souls. But since the scope
Must widen early, is it well to droop
For a few days consumed in loss and taint?
O pusillanimous Heart, be comforted,—
And, like a cheerful traveller, take the road,
Singing beside the hedge. What if the bread
Be bitter in thine inn, and thou unshod
To meet the flints?—At least it may be said,
'Because the way is *short,* I thank thee, God!'

DISCONTENT

*L*ight human nature is too lightly tost
And ruffled without cause; complaining on—
Restless with rest—until, being overthrown,
It learneth to lie quiet. Let a frost
Or a small wasp have crept to the innermost
Of our ripe peach: or let the wilful sun
Shine westward of our window—straight we run
A furlong's sigh as if the world were lost
But what time through the heart and through
   the brain
God hath transfixed us,—we, so moved before,
Attain to a calm. Ay, shouldering weights of pain,
We anchor in deep waters, safe from shore;
And hear, submissive, o'er the stormy main,
God's chartered judgments walk forevermore.

FUTURITY

And, O beloved voices, upon which
Ours passionately call, because ere long
Ye brake off in the middle of that song
We sang together softly, to enrich
The poor world with the sense of love, and witch
The heart out of things evil,—I am strong,
Knowing ye are not lost for aye among
The hills, with last year's thrush. God keeps a niche
In Heaven to hold our idols: and albeit
He brake them to our faces and denied
That our close kisses should impair their white,—
I know we shall behold them, raised complete,
The dust swept from their beauty,—glorified
New Memnons singing in the great God-light.

CONSOLATION

*A*ll are not taken! there are left behind
Living Beloveds, tender looks to bring,
And make the daylight still a happy thing,
And tender voices, to make soft the wind.
But if it were not so—if I could find
No love in all the world for comforting,
Nor any path but hollowly did ring,
Where 'dust to dust' the love from life disjoined—
And if before these sepulchres unmoving
I stood alone, (as some forsaken lamb
Goes bleating up the moors in weary dearth)
Crying 'Where are ye, O my loved and loving?'. . .
I know a Voice would sound, 'Daughter, I AM.
Can I suffice for HEAVEN, and not for earth?'

THE PRISONER

I count the dismal time by months and years,
Since last I felt the green sward under foot,
And the great breath of all things summer-mute
Met mine upon my lips. Now earth appears
As strange to me as dreams of distant spheres,
Or thoughts of Heaven we weep at. Nature's lute
Sounds on behind this door so closely shut,
A strange wild music to the prisoner's ears,
Dilated by the distance, till the brain
Grows dim with fancies which it feels too fine:
While ever, with a visionary pain,
Past the precluded senses, sweep and shine
Streams, forests, glades,—and many a golden train
Of sunlit hills, transfigured to Divine.

ADEQUACY

*N*ow by the verdure on thy thousand hills,
Beloved England,— doth the earth appear
Quite good enough for men to overbear
The will of God in, with rebellious wills!
We cannot say the morning sun fulfils
Ingloriously its course: nor that the clear
Strong stars without significance insphere
Our habitation. We, meantime, our ills
Heap up against this good; and lift a cry
Against this work-day world, this ill-spread feast,
As if ourselves were better certainly
Than what we come to. Maker and High Priest,
I ask thee not my joys to multiply,—
Only make me worthier of the least.

THE SERAPH AND POET

The seraph sings before the manifest
God-one, and in the burning of the Seven,
And with the full life of consummate Heaven
Heaving beneath him like a mother's breast
Warm with her first-born's slumber in that nest!
The poet sings upon the earth grave-riven:
Before the naughty world soon self-forgiven
For wronging him; and in the darkness prest
From his own soul by worldly weights. Even so,
Sing, seraph with the glory! Heaven is high—
Sing, poet with the sorrow! Earth is low.
The universe's inward voices cry
'Amen' to either song of joy and woe—
Sing seraph, poet, sing on equally.

A Thought for a Lonely Death-Bed

Inscribed to my Friend E.C.

If God compel thee to this destiny,
To die alone,—with none beside thy bed
To ruffle round with sobs thy last word said,
And mark with tears the pulses ebb from thee,—
Pray then alone—'O Christ, come tenderly!
By thy forsaken Sonship in the red
Drear wine-press,—by the wilderness outspread,—
And the lone garden where Thine agony
Fell bloody from thy brow,—by all of those
Permitted desolations, comfort mine!
No earthly friend being near me, interpose
No deathly angel 'twixt my face and Thine,
But stoop Thyself to gather my life's rose,
And smile away my mortal to Divine.

To George Sand
A Desire

*T*hou large-brained woman and large-hearted man,
Self-called George Sand! whose soul amid the lions
Of thy tumultuous senses, moans defiance,
And answers roar for roar as spirits can:
I would some miraculous thunder ran
Above the applauded circus, in appliance
Of thine own nobler nature's strength and science,
Drawing two pinions, white as wings of swan,
From thy strong shoulders, to amaze the place
With holier light! That thou to woman's claim,
And man's, might join beside the angel's grace
Of a pure genius sanctified from blame;
Till child and maiden pressed to thine embrace,
To kiss upon thy lips a stainless fame.

ℰ𝓍𝒶𝑔𝑔ℯ𝓇𝒶𝓉𝒾ℴ𝓃

We overstate the ills of life, and take
Imagination, given us to bring down
The choirs of singing angels overshone
By God's clear glory,— down our earth to rake
The dismal snows instead; flake following flake,
To cover all the corn. We walk upon
The shadow of hills across a level thrown,
And pant like climbers. Near the alderbrake
We sigh so loud, the nightingale within
Refuses to sing loud, as else she would.
O brothers! let us leave the shame and sin
Of taking vainly, in a plaintive mood,
The holy name of GRIEF!—holy herein,
That, by the grief of ONE, came all our good.

Mountaineer and Poet

*T*he simple goatherd, between Alp and sky,
Seeing his shadow in that awful tryst,
Dilated to a giant's on the mist,
Esteems not his own stature larger by
The apparent image, but more patiently
Strikes his staff down beneath his clenching fist—
While the snow-mountains lift their amethyst
And sapphire crowns of splendor, far and nigh,
Into the air around him. Learn from hence
Meek morals, all ye poets that pursue
Your way still onward up to eminence!
Ye are not great, because creation drew
Large revelations round your earliest sense,
Nor bright, because God's glory shines for you.

FINITE AND INFINITE

The wind sounds only in opposing straights,
The sea, beside the shore; man's spirit rends
Its quiet only up against the ends
Of wants and oppositions, loves and hates,
Where worked and worn by passionate debates,
And losing by the loss it apprehends
The flesh rocks round, and every breath it sends,
Is ravelled to a sigh. All tortured states
Suppose a straightened place. Jehovah Lord,
Make room for rest, around me! Out of sight
Now float me, of the vexing land abhorred,
Till, in deep calms of space, my soul may right
Her nature: shoot large sail on lengthening cord,
And rush exultant on the Infinite.

WORK AND
CONTEMPLATION

*T*he woman singeth at her spinning wheel
A pleasant chant, ballad or barcarolle;
She thinketh of her song, upon the whole,
Far more than of the flax; and yet the reel
Is full, and artfully her fingers feel
With quick adjustment, provident control,
The lines, too subtly twisted to unroll,
Out to a perfect thread. I hence appeal
To the dear Christian church—that we may do
Our Father's business in these temples mirk,
Thus swift and steadfast; thus intent and strong
While, thus, apart from toil, our souls pursue
Some high, calm, spheric tune, and prove our work
The better for the sweetness of our song.

BEREAVEMENT

When some Beloveds, 'neath whose eyelids lay
The sweet lights of my childhood, one by one
Did leave me dark before the natural sun,
And I astonished fell, and could not pray,
A thought within me to myself did say,
'Is God less God that *thou* art left undone?
Rise, worship, bless Him, in this sackcloth spun,
As in that purple!'—But I answered Nay!
What child his filial heart in words can loose,
If he behold his tender father raise
The hand that chastens sorely? can he choose
But sob in silence with an upward gaze?—
And *my* great Father, thinking fit to bruise,
Discerns in speechless tears, both prayer and praise.

HEAVEN AND EARTH

And there was silence in heaven for
the space of half-an-hour.
                              —Revelation

God, who, with thunders and great voices kept
Beneath thy throne, and stars most silver-paced
Along the inferior gyres, and open-faced
Melodious angels round;— canst intercept
Music with music;—yet, at will, has swept
All back, all back, (said he in Patmos placed,)
To fill the heavens with silence of the waste,
Which lasted half-an-hour!— Lo, I who have wept
All day and night, beseech thee by my tears,
And by that dread response of curse and groan
Men alternate across these hemispheres,
Vouchsafe us such a half-hour's hush alone,
In compensation for our stormy years!
As heaven has paused from song, let earth,
        from moan.

INSUFFICIENCY

*W*hen I attain to utter forth in verse
Some inward thought, my soul throbs audibly
Along my pulses, yearning to be free
And something farther, fuller, higher rehearse,
To the individual, true, and the universe.
In consummation of right harmony.
But, like a wind-exposed, distorted tree,
We are blown against for ever by the curse
Which breathes through nature. O, the world is weak
The effluence of each is false to all;
And what we best conceive, we fail to speak.
Wait, soul, until thine ashen garments fall!
And then resume thy broken strains and seek
Fit peroration, without let or thrall.

THE PROSPECT

*M*ethinks we do as fretful children do,
Leaning their faces on the window-pane
To sigh the glass dim with their own breath's stain,
And shut the sky and landscape from their view.
And thus, alas! since God the maker drew
A mystic separation 'twixt those twain,
The life beyond us, and our souls in pain,
We miss the prospect which we're called unto
By grief we're fools to use. Be still and strong
O man, my brother! hold thy sobbing breath,
And keep thy soul's large window pure from wrong,—
That so, as life's appointment issueth,
Thy vision may be clear to watch along
The sunset consummation-lights of death.

INCLUSIONS

Oh, wilt thou have my hand, Dear, to lie along
in thine?

As a little stone in a running stream, it seems to lie
and pine!

Now drop the poor pale hand, Dear, . . unfit to plight
with thine

Oh, wilt thou have my cheek, Dear, drawn closer to
thine own?

My cheek is white, my cheek is worn, by many a tear
run down.

Now leave a little space, Dear, lest it should wet thine
own.

Oh, must thou have my soul, Dear, commingled with
thy soul?—

Red grows the cheek, and warm the hand, . . the part
is in the whole! . .

Nor hands nor cheeks keep separate, when soul is
joined to soul. . .

Insufficiency

*T*here is no one beside thee, and no one above thee;
Thou standest alone, as the nightingale sings!
Yet my words that would praise thee are impotent
      things,
For none can express thee though all should
      approve thee!
I love thee so, Dear, that I only can love thee.
Say, what can I do for thee? . . . weary thee . . .
      grieve thee?
Lean on my shoulder . . . new burdens to add?
Weep my tears over thee . . . making thee sad?
Oh, hold me not—love me not? let me retrieve thee!
I love thee so, Dear, that I only can leave thee.

PAST AND FUTURE

*M*y future will not copy fair my past
On any leaf but Heaven's. Be fully done,
Supernal Will! I would not fain be one
Who, satisfying thirst and breaking fast
Upon the fulness of the heart, at last
Says no grace after meat. My wine hath run
Indeed out of my cup, and there is none
To gather up the bread of my repast
Scattered and trampled;—yet I find some good
In earth's green herbs and springs that bubble up
Clear from the darkling ground,—content until
I sit with angels before better food.
Dear Christ! when thy new vintage fills my cup,
This hand shall shake no more, nor that wine spill.

IRREPARABLENESS

I have been in the meadows all the day
And gathered there the nosegay that you see:
Singing within myself as bird or bee
When such do field-work on a morn of May:
But now I look upon my flowers — decay
Has met them in my hands more fatally
Because more warmly clasped; and sobs are free
To come instead of songs. What do you say,
Sweet counsellors, dear friends? that I should go
Back straightway to the fields, and gather more?
Another, sooth, may do it,— but not I:
My heart is very tired— my strength is low—
My hands are full of blossoms plucked before,
Held dead within them till myself shall die.

TEARS

*T*hank God, bless God, all ye who suffer not
More grief than ye can weep for. That is well—
That is light grieving! lighter, none befell,
Since Adam forfeited the primal lot.
Tears! what are tears? The babe weeps in its cot,
The mother singing; at her marriage bell
The bride weeps; and before the oracle
Of high-faned hills, the poet has forgot
Such moisture on his cheeks. Thank God for grace,
Ye who weep only! If, as some have done,
Ye grope tear-blinded in a desert place,
And touch but tombs,—look up! Those tears will run
Soon in long rivers down the lifted face,
And leave the vision clear for stars and sun.

AN APPREHENSION

If all the gentlest-hearted friends I know
Concentred in one heart their gentleness,
That still grew gentler, till its pulse was less
For life than pity, I should yet be slow
To bring my own heart nakedly below
The palm of such a friend, that he should press
Motive, condition, means, appliances,
My false ideal joy and fickle wo,
Out full to light and knowledge. I should fear
Some plait between the brows—some rougher chime
In the free voice. . . . O angels, let the flood
Of bitter scorn dash on me! Do ye hear
What *I* say, who bear calmly all the time
This everlasting face to face with GOD?

SUBSTITUTION

When some beloved voice that was to you
Both sound and sweetness, faileth suddenly,
And silence against which you dare not cry,
Aches round you like a strong disease and new—
What hope? what help? what music will undo
That silence to your sense? Not friendship's sigh—
Nor reason's subtle count! Not melody
Of viols, nor of pipes that Faunus blew—
Not songs of poets, nor of nightingales,
Whose hearts leap upward through the cypress trees
To the clear moon; nor yet the spheric laws
Self-chanted,—nor the angel's sweet All hails,
Met in the smile of God. Nay, none of these.
Speak Thou, availing Christ!—and fill this pause.

Love

*W*e cannot live, except thus mutually
We alternate, aware or unaware,
The reflex act of life: and when we bear
Our virtue onward most impulsively,
Most full of invocation, and to be
Most instantly compellant, certes, there
We live most life, whoever breathes most air
And counts his dying years by sun and sea.
But when a soul, by choice and conscience, doth
Throw out her full force on another soul,
The conscience and the concentration both
Make mere life, Love. For Life in perfect whole
And aim consummated, is Love in sooth,
As nature's magnet-heat rounds pole with pole.

Hiram Powers' Greek Slave

*T*hey say Ideal Beauty cannot enter
The house of anguish. On the threshold stands
An alien Image with enshackled hands,
Called the Greek Slave: as if the artist meant her,
(That passionless perfection which he lent her,
Shadowed not darkened where the sill expands)
To, so, confront man's crimes in different lands
With man's ideal sense. Pierce to the centre,
Art's fiery finger!—and break up ere long
The serfdom of this world! Appeal, fair stone,
From God's pure heights of beauty, against man's
    wrong!
Catch up in thy divine face, not alone
East griefs but west,—and strike and shame the strong,
By thunders of white silence, overthrown.

LIFE

$\mathcal{E}$ach creature holds an insular point in space:
Yet what man stirs a finger, breathes a sound,
But all the multitudinous beings round
In all the countless worlds, with time and place
For their conditions, down to the central base,
Thrill, haply, in vibration and rebound,
Life answering life across the vast profound,
In full antiphony, by a common grace!
I think, this sudden joyaunce which illumes
A child's mouth sleeping, unaware may run
From some soul newly loosened from earth's tombs:
I think, this passionate sigh, which half-begun
I stifle back, may reach and stir the plumes
Of God's calm angel standing in the sun.

THE SOUL'S EXPRESSION

With stammering lips and insufficient sound
I strive and struggle to deliver right
That music of my nature, day and night
With dream and thought and feeling interwound,
And inly answering all the senses round
With octaves of a mystic depth and height
Which step out grandly to the infinite
From the dark edges of the sensual ground!
This song of soul I struggle to outbear
Through portals of the sense, sublime and whole,
And utter all myself into the air:
But if I did it,—as the thunder-roll
Breaks its own cloud,—my flesh would perish there,
Before that dread apocalypse of soul.

THE POET

*T*he poet hath the child's sight in his breast,
And sees all *new*. What oftenest he has viewed
He views with the first glory. Fair and good
Pall never on him, at the fairest, best,
But stand before him holy and undressed
In week-day false conventions, such as would
Drag other men down from the altitude
Of primal types, too early dispossessed.
Why, God would tire of all his heaven as soon
As thou, O godlike, childlike poet, didst,
Of daily and nightly sights of sun and moon!
And therefore hath He set thee in the midst,
Where men may hear thy wonder's ceaseless tune,
And praise His world for ever as thou bidst.

Index of First Lines